UP 'N' UNDER

First published in Great Britain in 1998 by
Chameleon Books
76 Dean Street
London W1V 5HA

CIP data for this title is available from the British Library

ISBN 0 233 99356 8

Book and jacket design by Generation Studio

Origination by Digicol Link, London

Printed in Spain by Graficas Zamudio Printek, S.A.L.

André Deutsch Ltd is a VCI plc company

ACKNOWLEDGEMENTS:

Special thanks to Linda Baritski, Paul Sudbury,
Rob Stevens, Andrew Varley, Mary Killingsworth, Mark Peacock,
Caroline Warde, Lucy and Ali Milich,
Joanne Meeks, all at Generation Associates,
Louise Dixon – and the man who made it all possible, Tim Forrester.

PHOTOGRAPH ACKNOWLEDGEMENTS

Allsport Press
cover photo, 6, 7, 12, 13, 17-25, 31, 38,
54, 56-58, 60, 61, 66, 72, 73, 76, 86,
91, 94, 98, 99, 102, 107-109

Varely Picture Agency Pages
8, 10, 11, 16, 26-41, 44-53, 63, 64, 67, 68,
79, 82-89, 92, 93, 97, 100, 101

DEDICATED TO:

'Big' Johnny Taylor, 'S**t Hot' Price
and other terrors of the Southern Amateurs...

"I can identify with many of the pictures in this book, having been pile-drived into the mud by some Neanderthal forward more times than I care to remember. League's like that – the tackles you have to make, the knocks you have to take, endlessly – you just get up, dust yourself down and get on with it. So why, oh why, do we do it? I'll tell you – because it's bloody marvellous."

Keep Smiling

JOHN BENTLEY

"BLOODY 'ELL, I THOUGHT MAVIS WAS AT THE HAIRDRESSERS TODAY."

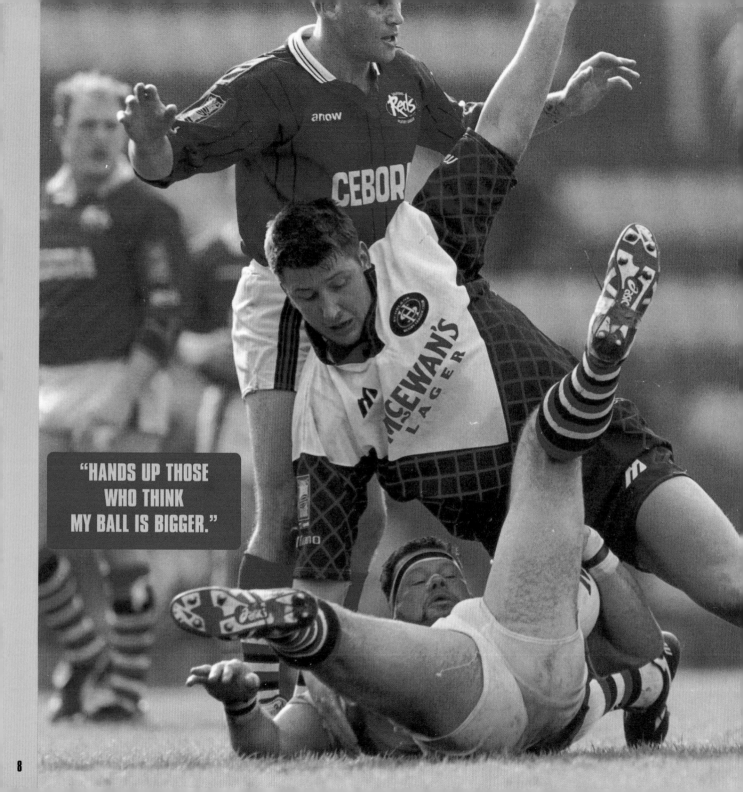

"HANDS UP THOSE
WHO THINK
MY BALL IS BIGGER."

NOT YOUR NIGHT, SON

Looking For A Place To Hide

In the history book of rugby league, Don Fox deserves his own special place, for his is a heartbreaking story. The 1968 Challenge Cup Final between Fox's Wakefield Trinity side and Leeds was a cliff-hanger watched by a packed Wembley stadium and millions more on TV. The match rested on Fox's shoulders after Trinity had scored a try to move within one point of Leeds at 11-10 down. A useful forward and goal kicker, Fox's conversion from fairly straight on to the posts should have been a formality to wrap the cup up for his club. It may have been the pressure of the situation and all those watching, or it may have been the pitch conditions, but Fox slipped as he approached the kick and the ball squirted wide. Fox buried his head in his hands, Leeds players danced in celebration of victory. Even so, Don Fox received the Lance Todd trophy for man of the match. It's a cruel game.

> 'I think you enjoy the game more if you don't know the rules. Anyway, you're on the same wavelength as referees.'
> Jonathan Davies

> 'It's the sort of thing you take on the chin.'
> Va'iga Tuigamala when asked about a knee injury

NAME THE OPPOSITION
PLAYER HONKING
IN THE CUP

"YEAH, WELL I'M A BETTER SHEEP SHAGGER THAN YOU'LL EVER BE!" (GREAT BRITAIN v NEW ZEALAND SLANGING MATCH)

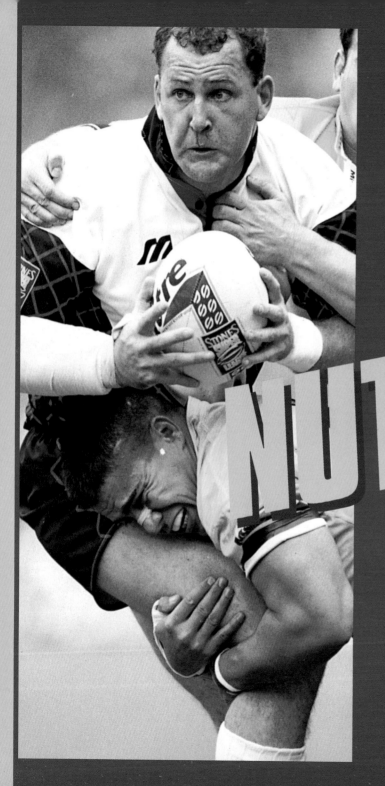

NUTTERS!

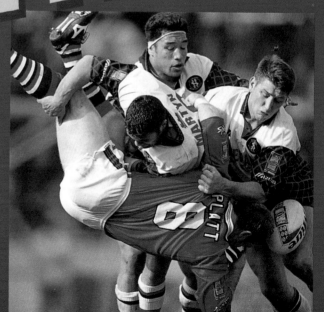

> 'Rugby league is a game of grit and passion. It was born out of controversy and has had its fair share of ups and downs ever since. Yet nothing has stopped its popularity growing from those small beginnings in the north of England.'
> Rodney Walker – RFL

> 'I've often thought that if the Inland Revenue were ever to make public the tax returns of rugby union players, British Rail would have to lay on extra north-bound trains to cope with the rush.'
> Jonathan Davies

> 'Northern Union players can only play with Rugby Union players in bona fide Naval and Military teams in which there are Northern Union players. Munitions workers cannot be regarded as Naval and Military players. These rulings only apply during the war.'
> Rugby Football Union decree for World War II

Safe Hands

The 1976 Grand Final at the Sydney Cricket Ground between Parramatta and Manly will not hold many fond memories for Parramatta winger Neville Glover. With his team down 11-10 and with just 12 minutes to go, Parramatta switched their tactics and decided to take the ball away from the forwards and out to the backs. It was slung out wide to the waiting Glover, eager for his first touch of the ball. The line was just a few yards away and the defence was nowhere. A Glover try would probably seal Parramatta's first ever grand final win. But Glover dropped the ball, and with that fumble went any hope of Parramatta glory.

Woods' Woe

The 1980 Challenge Cup final was a derby match between Hull and neighbours Hull Kingston Rovers. Not unexpectedly there was the odd bit of rough house stuff, but none more costly than when Hull's Paul Woods needlessly fouled HKR's Steve Hubbard as Hubbard grounded the ball for a try after just eight minutes. Hubbard himself missed the conversion, but gleefully accepted the chance to add extra points from the penalty awarded in front of the posts for Woods' foul. HKR went on to win 10-5.

> 'League is much, much more physical than Union, and that's before anyone started breaking the rules. '
> Adrian Hadley

Silly Billy

Rochdale's one and only Challenge Cup victory came in 1922, but it was a close run thing. Rochdale's lead was eroded to 10-9 by a Bob Jones try for Hull, leaving kicker Billy Stone a relatively simple conversion to seal victory. He missed, and to rub salt in the wounds 12 months later Hull lost in the final again, this time to Leeds.

> 'Anyone who's seen the Wigan players stripped has been faced with the raw truth of the matter... No time for male modelling...'
> Colin Welland (Observer 1995)

Life's A Riot

English referee Billy Thompson has few friends in France after officiating in a European Championship game between France and England at Narbonne in 1980. England won a tight game 4-2, but Thompson disallowed a late French try for a forward pass – a decision which didn't sit too well with the home crowd. Come the final whistle Thompson had to sprint for the safety of his dressing room where he stayed under police guard for two hours while the crowd rioted.

THE MAN IN THE MIDDLE
How Long Gone, Ref?

The match between Great Britain and New South Wales on the 1954 tour of Australia erupted into a huge and uncontrollable brawl. So bad was the fighting that the referee, Aubrey Oxford, simply walked off the pitch and abandoned the game after 56 minutes.

> 'Bradford didn't realise how good he was, he was always tough to deal with financially, but you always knew you would get value for money. He was the ultimate big game player who would do the business no matter how hard the challenge. He was tough physically and mentally. I have never met anyone with such a strong will. Ellery was not the biggest or the fastest, but the composite picture was one of a supreme athlete. Pound for pound, I'd rate him as the best player of all time.'
> Wigan chairman Jack Robinson on Ellery Hanley

"I GOT A TELLY TUBBIE FOR CHRISTMAS!"

Walk Out

The premiership match of May 1982 between Hull Kingston Rovers and Bradford Northern was a bad tempered affair. Brawls, high tackles and skirmishes led to a spate of sendings off by hapless referee Robin Whitfield. Approaching the mid-point of the second half, with five players already enjoying an early bath, Bradford captain Jeff Grayshon was asked by the referee to join them in the changing room. Obviously not pleased, Grayshon appeared to throw the ball at referee Whitfield and then told his team to leave the field with him. The remaining Bradford players trooped down the tunnel, into the dressing room and locked the door. The game was abandoned.

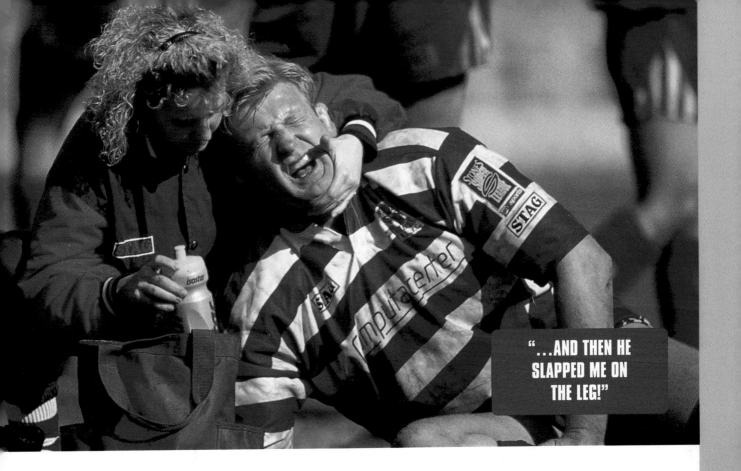

"...AND THEN HE SLAPPED ME ON THE LEG!"

Allez France

French referee Guy Cattaneo proved the catalyst for using neutral officials at international games.

Refereeing the 1981 England v France game at Headingley, Cattaneo showed a distinct favouritism to his country's team, allowing them great leniency with offside and other offences, while nipping any promising English moves in the bud with a shrill blast of the whistle. Even a 'polite but serious discussion about rule interpretation' with a British official at half-time had no effect, and France not surprisingly won 5-1.

BREAK

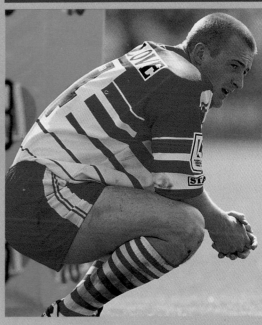

ING WIND

BREAKING WIND

BREAKING
WIND

BREAKING WIND

BREAKING WIND

BREAKING WIND

BREAKING WIND

BREAKING WIND

"CAREFUL WITH MY CAMI-KNICKERS, BOYS."

"SO THAT'S WHERE THE TOILET ROLL WENT!"

EXCUSE ME, IS THIS THE QUEUE FOR "101 DALMATIONS"?

'As far as I can see rugby league football is easy to understand. A match lasts for 80 minutes and everybody goes home with a piece of the other side.'
Cartoon 1927

'It's Great Britain in the all-white strip with the red and blue V, the dark shorts and the dark stockings.'
Ray French

'It was the first time I had seen seagulls at a match... with the teams in one half of the field and the gulls in the other.'
Eddie Waring remarks on bad weather conditions at a New Zealand v Britain game.

Lawless Lawler

Picture the scene. A close test match – Britain leading Australia in Sydney by 17-13 with two minutes to go. Then Australia score in the corner to close the gap to one point. The conversion will win the game for the Aussies, but it's a tough one from the touch line. Until, that is, English-hating referee Darcy Lawler tells the Australian kicker he can place the ball bang in front of the posts if he so wishes. The kicker, Ken Irvine, not one to look a gift horse in the mouth, did so, kicked the conversion and won the match 18-17. True story – 1962.

THE INVISIBLE MAN CAUGHT STAMPING AN OPPOSITION PLAYER

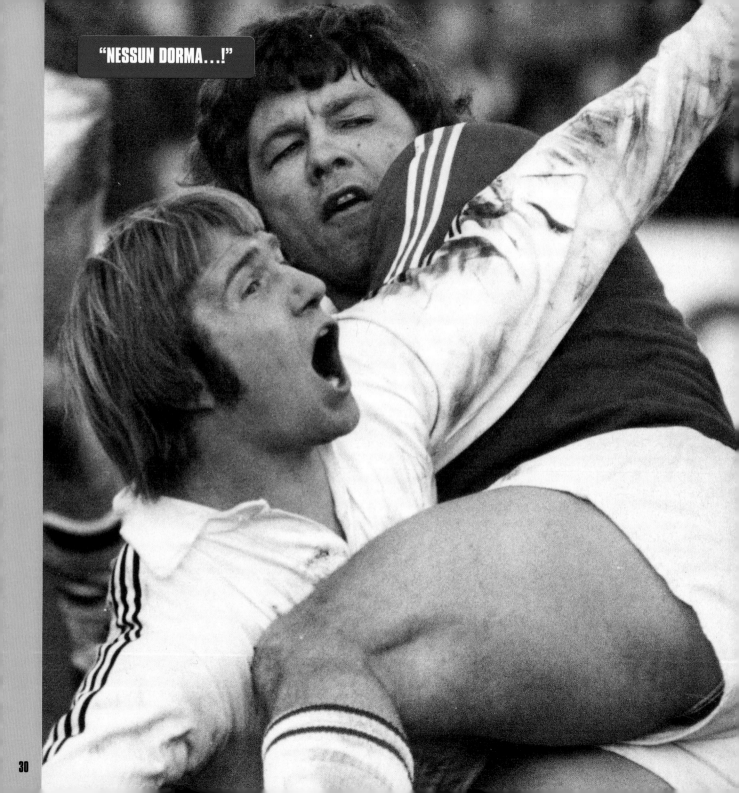

"NESSUN DORMA...!"

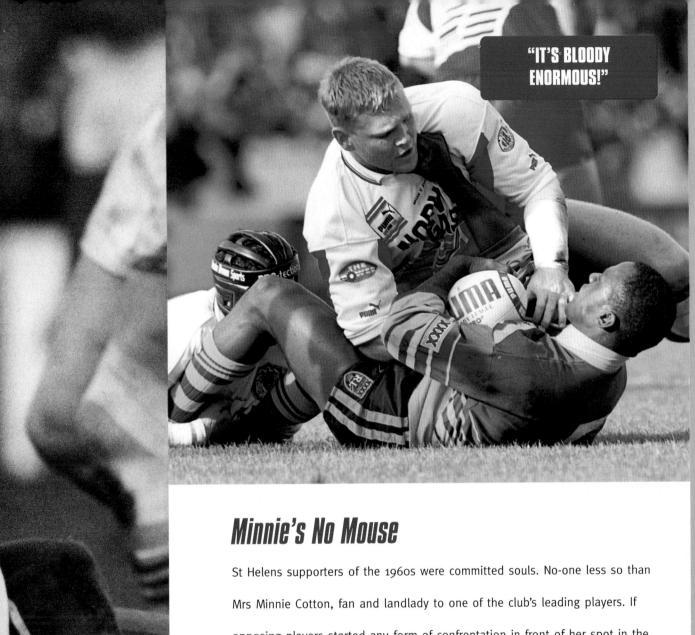

"IT'S BLOODY ENORMOUS!"

Minnie's No Mouse

St Helens supporters of the 1960s were committed souls. No-one less so than
Mrs Minnie Cotton, fan and landlady to one of the club's leading players. If
opposing players started any form of confrontation in front of her spot in the
main stand, Mrs Cotton (well in to her 50s) was not averse to wading in and
handing out a few lusty blows with her handbag or umbrella.

HOW MANY CELEBRITIES CAN YOU SPOT? HERE'S A FEW TO BE GOING ON WITH:
ERIC MORECOMBE, DAVID STEELE, JIMMY SAVILLE, ENA SHARPLES, BARONESS THATCHER...

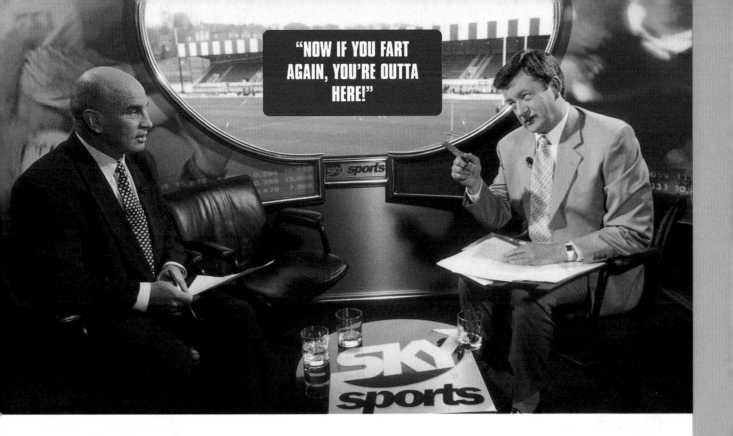

"NOW IF YOU FART AGAIN, YOU'RE OUTTA HERE!"

'The Sydney Cricket Ground Hill is the stuff of which Pom nightmares are made. When a small child in the north of England misbehaves outrageously, parents have been known to threaten to send him there on grand final day, and let nature take its course. Just as surely as we know that Dover has white cliffs and Wigan a pier, so we know that no-one comes back alive from The Hill.' George Dunkerley in Rugby League Week on the hottest vantage point to watch an Australian grand final match.

ROUGH STUFF
Cross Off

New Zealand's W Cross has the dubious distinction of being the first sending off in a rugby league international. He got his marching orders ten minutes from the end of the third Test between Northern Union and New Zealand in 1908. For this honour Cross was suspended for just one week.

JUST IN CASE JOMAH LOMU CHANGES CODE AND COUNTRY...

No, After You

Australia beat New Zealand 26-20 in June 1985, but few will remember the match for the scoreline. Instead the headlines focused on the violence that broke out in the dying minutes – particularly the sight of players Kevin Tamati of New Zealand and Greg Dowling of Australia scrapping their way off the field and almost into the crowd after being sin-binned.

'The northern he-man world of rugby league went to town yesterday, and enthusiastic Londoners voted it a smash hit.'
Alan Thompson, Daily Express

It's Not Easy, Boyo

The transition of rugby union player to league is not always a smooth one. Welsh scrum half David Bishop finished his debut for Hull Kingston Rovers in hospital, and another great Welsh scrum half, Terry Holmes lasted just 13 minutes of his debut for Bradford Northern before having to leave the field with a shoulder injury which would dog the rest of his league career.

...AND HIS SHORTS.

Love Match

The 1970 World Cup final between England and Australia was dubbed the 'Battle of Leeds' because of the continuous rough stuff. The match finished with Australia's Billy Smith and England's Syd Hynes exchanging headbutts and punches across the touchline as they were sent off, and then a stand up brawl between the two teams. Australia won 12-7.

> 'Shaun Edwards has happy memories of Wembley.
> On his last appearance here he received a fractured cheekbone.'
> Ray French

Take That

A 1976 semi-final between Wests and Redc[...] in Brisbane was a rumbustuous affair. Redcliffe prop John Barber was sent off in [...] very first minute and then war broke out. [...] big brawl saw players exchanging haymake[...] near the main grandstand fence. Unable to [...] control herself, a lady spectator also got involved, lashing out with a bright red handbag, aiming lusty blows at players regardless of which side they were playing [...]

THE DAY THE EARTH MOVED...FOR HIM!

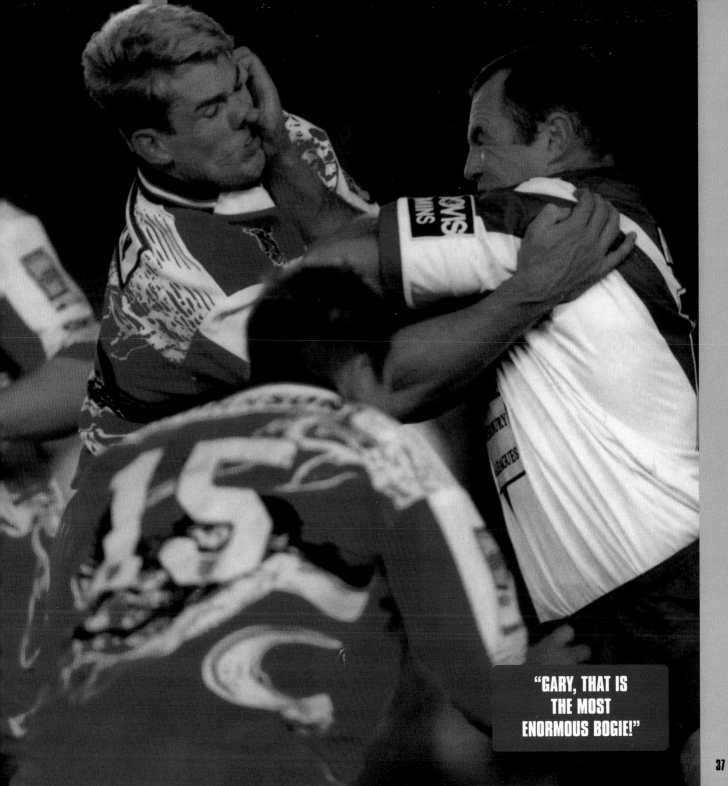

"GARY, THAT IS THE MOST ENORMOUS BOGIE!"

GARY SCHOFIELD BEING ATTACKED BY A TWO HEADED KIWI.

THINK BEFORE YOU SPEAK
Me And My Big Mouth

France toured Australia in 1951 and one Sydney newspaper rather harshly

opined that the French were not up to the playing standards of the Australians,

and they should be 'sent home on the first available plane.' The French then

went on to beat the Australians 29-15.

"GUESS WHO'S BUYING THE BEER TONIGHT!"

Marked Man

Manly prop Martin Bella carried a price on his head for the 1991 semi-final match with North Sydney. Bella's comments prior to the game, calling Norths a 'terrible side' led to a $200 incentive being placed for anyone who could knock Bella out during the game.

'Soccer, the game I have loved for 40 years, is on the run, threatened with exposure of its dull and flabby attitudes by the strident virility of rugby league.'
David Miller, Daily Express

'I'm 49, I've had a brain haemorrhage and a triple bypass and I could still go out and play a reasonable game of rugby union. But I wouldn't last 30 seconds in rugby league.'
Graham Lowe, former Wigan coach

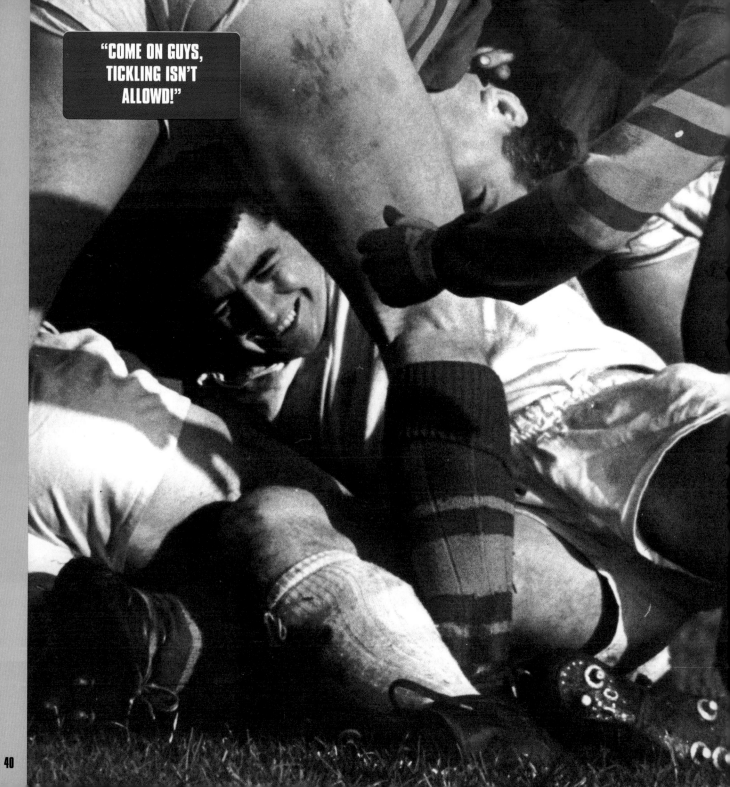

"COME ON GUYS, TICKLING ISN'T ALLOWD!"

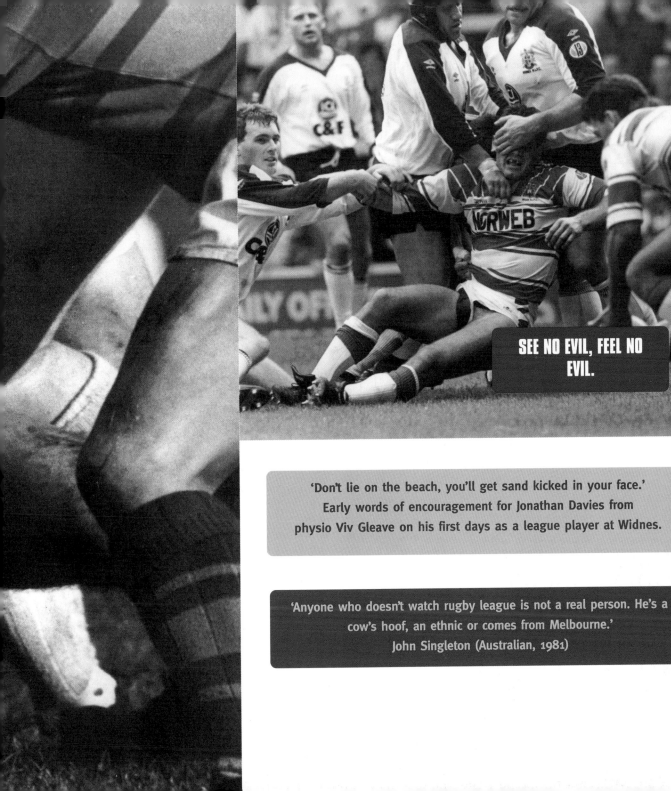

SEE NO EVIL, FEEL NO EVIL.

'Don't lie on the beach, you'll get sand kicked in your face.'
Early words of encouragement for Jonathan Davies from
physio Viv Gleave on his first days as a league player at Widnes.

'Anyone who doesn't watch rugby league is not a real person. He's a
cow's hoof, an ethnic or comes from Melbourne.'
John Singleton (Australian, 1981)

Wise Words

Eddie Waring was convinced that Britain would win the 1957 World Cup in Australia and therefore retain the trophy first won in 1954. 'It's hardly worth paying the cost of the big trophy by taking it to Sydney. It should be so easy for Britain to win with a side like this against the sort of team Australia can field.'

Needless to say the Australians beat Britain 30-6 on the way to winning the Cup on home soil.

'Shaun Edwards has happy memories of Wembley. On his last appearance here he received a fractured cheekbone.'
Ray French

TOUGHING IT OUT
One-Armed And Dangerous

Rugby league is a hard game. During the second Test between the British Lions and Australia in Brisbane in 1958, the Lions' captain, Alan Prescott, broke his arm after only three minutes of the game. After 17 minutes Lions stand-off Dave Bolton left the field with a broken collar bone and three other Lions needed hospital treatment after the game. Prescott, however, played out the rest of the game with one arm hanging limp by his side and actually led the Lions to a 25-18 victory.

"LOOK, YOU CAN SEE RIGHT OUT HIS NOSE."

"YOU'VE GOT A BIT OF GRIT JUST...THERE!"

"IT REALLY HURTS, ELLERY, PLEASE KISS IT BETTER."

'When I called acquaintances of Ellery Hanley for quotes about this Garboesque sportsman, I was met by an omerta, which any Mafia Godfather would have envied. People tread warily around Ellery Hanley. The road to his door is strewn with eggshells.'
Michael Parkinson, *Sporting Profiles*

'We had carte blanche to do what we wanted. Darcy hated Poms... he hated them with a vengeance. He once told me he would do everything in his power to ensure Australian victories against them.'
1958 Australian captain Ian Walsh sings the praises of referee Darcy Lawler.

'The main difference between playing League and Union is that now I get my hangovers on Monday instead of Sunday.'
Tom David

'Zavos's first law of player payments: no rugby league player is worth even half of what he is paid. Zavos's second law: no former rugby union player is worth a quarter of what he asks for to return to the code.'
Spire Zavos,
Sydney Morning Herald

'The freedom of the contract system was taken by a lot of players as a charter for greed.'
RFL chief executive Maurice Lindsay just a few years before taking Murdoch's Super League millions.

'Eddie Waring has done as much for the image of our sport as Cyril Smith would do for hang-gliding.'
Reg Bowden

AND YOU THINK THE TELLYTUBBIES LOOK STUPID...

ALL THE 1'S, LEGS 11.

"BOY, DO YOU GUYS SMELL!"

Man Of Steel, Jaw Of Glass

'When you're running with the ball try to run towards a back instead of a forward, pick the man who's going to tackle you and pick a small one if you can.' Stuart Evans offers Jonathan Davies advice.

Hull Kingston Rovers half-back Roger Millward sustained four broken jaws over the duration of his career, including one at the Challenge Cup Final in 1981 which he played on with to help Rovers win the trophy.

"BLOODY-ELL, YOU NEED ODOR EATERS!"

Backs To The Wall

The Rorke's Drift Test Match between the Northern Union and Australia in Sydney in 1914 goes down in the history books as one of the all-time great matches. The third and deciding Test of the series was a story of rearguard bravery of the Brits against seemingly impossible odds. Northern Union winger Frank Williams twisted his leg after just two minutes and eventually had to leave the field. Leading 9-3 at half-time, the Brits lost a forward with a broken collar bone, and then another player with concussion, leaving them with 10 men against 13. Remarkably, the Northern Union side not only held out and repelled Australia's continuous attacks, but scored again and won 14-6.

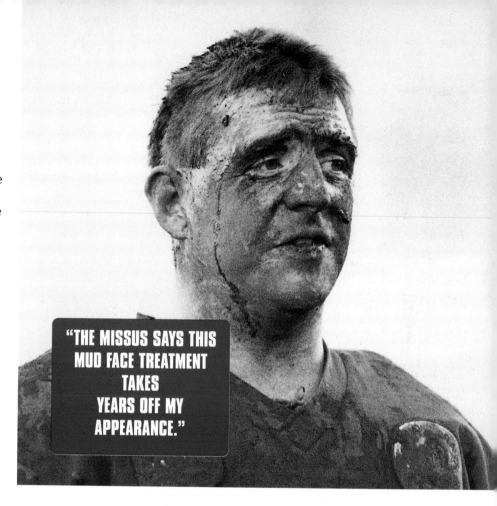

"THE MISSUS SAYS THIS MUD FACE TREATMENT TAKES YEARS OFF MY APPEARANCE."

The game won its nickname after the heroic rearguard action of 82 soldiers against 4000 Zulu warriors at Rorke's Drift in 1879.

"QUIET LADS,
HERE HE COMES."

51

"CRIKEY, IT'S A SHARK!"

TOURISTS
First Class Tickets

In August 1908 Australia set out to tour Britain for the first time – and with the squad cooped up on a liner for the six week voyage some players worked on their fitness by shovelling coal into the ship's furnaces.

Skippy Doesn't Last The Pace

The 1908 Australian touring party somehow procured a live kangaroo to act as a mascot to the team throughout the tour. It was not a successful tour, financially a failure and the Australians lost most of their games. And the kangaroo mascot died before the tour was completed.

"NEXT YEAR I'M ELIGIBLE FOR A SPONSORED CAR."

> If I'm injured during a game, I never let my opponent know. I don't even tell my team-mates.
> Ellery Hanley

Winning Isn't Everything — Official

Stipulation sent out by Northern Union to clubs when nominating players to tour abroad for the first time in 1910: 'In submitting such nominations they trust that you will only send the names of players who will do the honour to the Union both on and off the field of play, as it is their wish at the end of tour to have secured the reputation of not only having shown the best football, but of having sent out the best behaved and most gentlemanly team that has toured Australasia.'

We're Hard, Us

The touring New Zealand party of 1926/27 was not the happiest of squads, primarily due to the presence of manager E H Mair. He insisted that his wife travel with the squad as an official, and her role was to lead the fearsome All Black team on to the pitch for each match carrying a flag of New Zealand in one hand and a fluffy, cuddly Kiwi toy in the other.

Scary, eh?

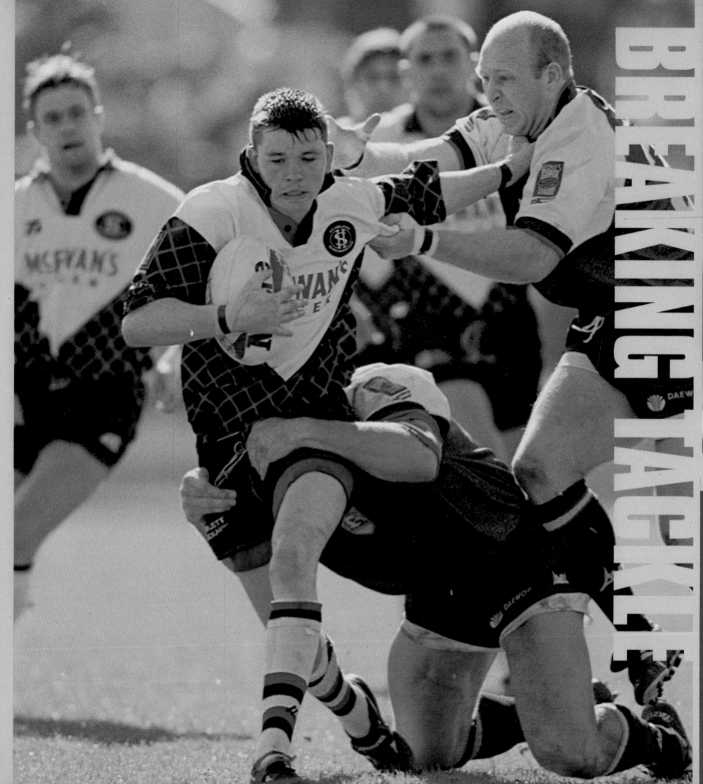

BREAKING TACKLE

BREAKING TACKLE

BREAKING TACKLE

BREAKING TACKLE

BREAKING TACKLE

BREAKING TACKLE

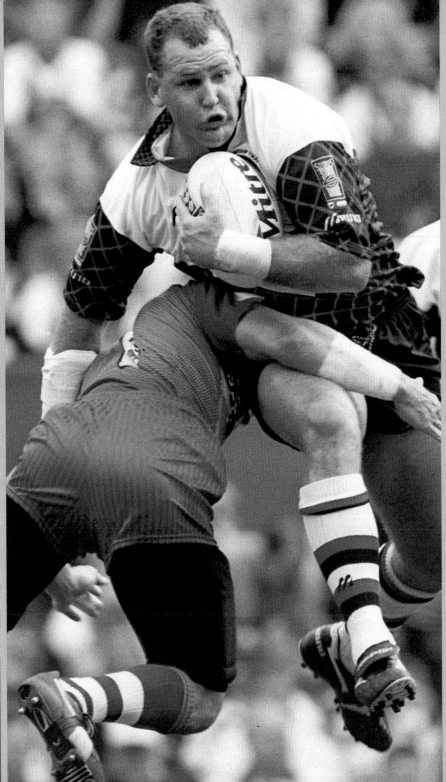

> 'It's pointless beating about the bush.
> It's the same old story – the Aussies are better players. They come from a better rugby league environment, and it's getting sickening. We've never won a series in this land since 1959, and it's getting to be a bloody worn-out gramophone record.'
> Maurice Lindsay after a 1997 defeat against Australia.

> 'Human elephants like Ian Van Bellen were tramping over the grass once graced by Johnny Haynes and George Best ...
> and 9,554 mums, dads and kids were loving every minute of it ... there wasn't a hooligan in sight.'
> Peter Blatt, Daily Star

> Rugby league is 'the toughest game yet invented on planet Earth.'
> Michael Parkinson

Going Our Way?

A British side was despatched to tour Australia in 1946, but a lack of transport meant the players, officials and journalists (including Eddie Waring) had to hitch a ride on the aircraft carrier HMS Indomitable which was sailing from Plymouth to Fremantle. This was, incidentally, the first touring party to be issued with jockstraps in their kit.

"CORKIN' PAIR OF BOOTS, LUV."

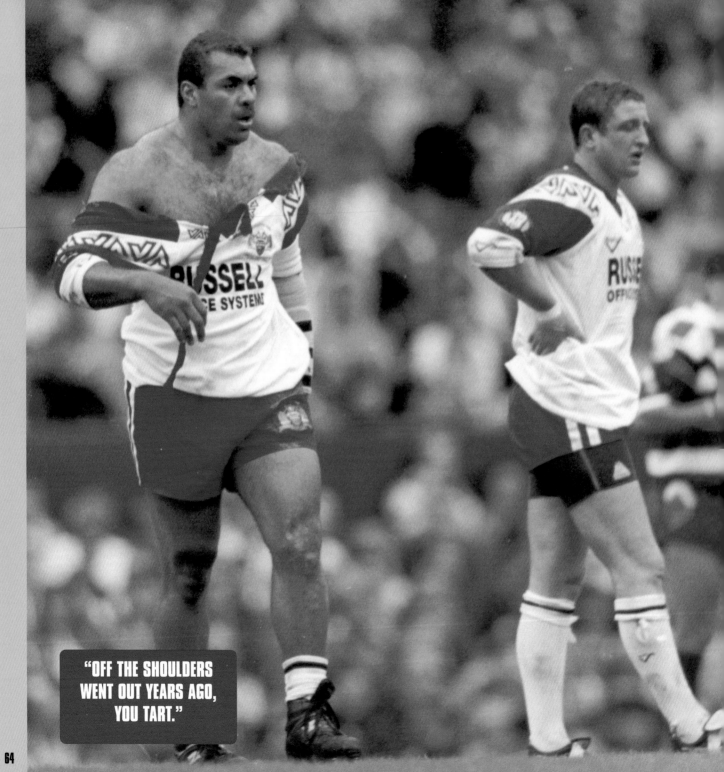

"OFF THE SHOULDERS
WENT OUT YEARS AGO,
YOU TART."

Flying Fears

The 1946 touring party down under became the first rugby league tourists to travel by air when they flew by boat plane from Sydney to Auckland. Just to be on the safe side, though, the squad divided itself evenly between three separate planes in case of accidents.

Watts Up?

Leeds forward Elijah Watts counted the cost of his attack on Batley's Wattie Davies as the pair left the pitch after a game in 1904. Watts was fined £1 and suspended for 10 days after a court case brought by Batley police.

GENERAL STORIES
Keep It Shut

In 1897 the Northern Union, obviously concerned with rowdy behaviour from the terraces, issued a warning that spectators found guilty of manhandling match officials, or worse still of using foul language, would be handed over to the police.

The success of the ultimatum was fairly limited, however. For example, later that year Morecambe found use of their ground suspended for two weeks after club officials hurled abuse at the match referee.

Page 58 *

ROUND

Redgr
and c
are
at

OFFIAH COMES OFF WORSE IN BRAWL WITH HAIRDRESSER

By JOHN DRAYTON

WAKEFIELD TRINITY moved four points clear at the top of rugby league's st. Division yesterday by overwhelming 64-8 at Belle Vue — their biggest season.

were celebrating a superb 12-try rest rivals Hull KR were sur-mid-table Whitehaven, ock inspired Trinity's ury-hit Widnes by the campaign an-of-the-tries

FIAH COMES OFF WORSE IN BRAWL WITH HIMSELF

By John Whalley

ve signed St Hel-
tt Goldspink for
Goldspink, who
e up against
sea on July
n in January
ns contract

I am very
ned for
mediate
hem in
lelens

last
ear-
s-
n
z

a
Former Auckland Warrior
us Maleotoa-Brown scored a
ce of tries for the Cumbri-
while Rovers' Papua New
ea half-back Stanley
the league's leading try-
landed his 24th touch-
f the season, surpass-
eason's tally.
climbed back into
e with a 24-18 win
le, who stay bot-
table despite a
ries from winger

were con-
th successive
hley gained
away win
-18 success

Larvin
minutes

Australian winger Josh
Bostock led the way for
Wakefield in their third win
of the season over the strug-
gling Vikings. He scored his
second hat-trick of the campaign, while hooker Roy
Southernwood and man-of-
the-match Andy Fisher each
collected two tries. Garen
Casey contributed 20 points
with a try and eight goals to
bring up his double century
and move into fourth place in
the leading scorers list.

Hull KR travelled to Cum-
bria with just one defeat in
nine games, but Whiteha-
ven's players responded to
the call of coach Stan Martin,
who described the fixture as
a "must-win game".

"GIVE US A PIGGY BACK MATE, ME TOOTSIES ARE GETTING COLD."

At A Canter

Wigan's South African winger of the 1920s, Attie Van Heerden, holds a place in the history books following the 1924 Challenge Cup Final at Rochdale.

Over 40,000 people paid to get into the game, but the stadium was hopelessly overcrowded, and policing spectators became a nightmare. Mounted police galloped up and down the touchlines throughout the game, and crowd surges onto the pitch were regular. During one such invasion, Van Heerden picked up a crossfield kick and sidestepped a moving police horse on his way to scoring beneath the posts as Wigan ran out winners by 21-4.

Cold Front

Weather hit rugby league badly in the great freeze of 1962/63. In the 69 days between 22nd December 1962 and 2nd March 1963, only seven of the scheduled league fixtures were actually played and completed.

Snow Joke

Does live television have a detrimental affect on crowd attendances? Wigan thought so in 1966, and refused to play their Challenge Cup tie against Bradford Northern in front of the cameras. For this they were fined £500 – and then, ironically, the match was postponed because of snow.

Er, Mr Smith?

A major signing for Fulham in the
early 1980s was speedy Moroccan
winger Hussain M'Barki, who played
for the French club Cahors. M'Barki
was signed for £25,000, having
appeared in several trial games
under the more anglicised
pseudonym of Des Smith.

Man's Stuff

The boom of the 1980s carried the
appeal of rugby league far and
wide. Even the Isle of Man
tabled a proposal in 1983 to stage
matches on its turf, but the offer
was declined.

"GET OFF! MY MUMMY TOLD ME ABOUT NAUGHTY MEN LIKE YOU."

71

A Hooker's Lot Is Not A Happy One

With an edict issued to referees to tidy up scrummaging in the 1981/82 season, the front rows found themselves in the spotlight, particularly hookers. In the first month of the season, 14 hookers were sent off, and at one disciplinary committee meeting in September, the usual suspects called in included 10 hookers. In a cup clash between Featherstone Rovers and Bradford Northern, referee Stan Wall dismissed both hookers. Gary Hale took over the hooking duties for Bradford, then got sent off, too.

Short Stuff

A match between Runcorn and Broughton Rangers in March 1913, which Runcorn won on the day, was declared void because the pitch was found to be too short.

'As for the ball, I never looked like getting anywhere near it. The boys were trying to let me get my bearings before they introduced anything as complicated as the ball into my thinking. Whichever side of the heel I lined up on, they played it the other way. This went on for 10 minutes and I was feeling more like a formation dancer than a rugby player.'
Early days for Jonathan Davies.

'And there's Kevin Ward raising his crutch to the fans.'
Ray French

COME ON LADS, YOU'RE NOT TAKING THIS GAME SERIOUSLY.

Sinners Repent

British rugby league welcomed the sin bin on 1st January 1983.

A New Game Is Born

The official birth of rugby league is taken as the 29th August 1895 when 21 representatives of the northern rugby football clubs met in the George Hotel in Huddersfield and decided to resign from the London-based Rugby Football Union, the governing body of their sport. The Northern Rugby Football Union, from which the modern game of rugby league would subsequently evolve, was formed.

'It's not Terry Holmes that Bradford Northern need – it's Sherlock.'
Alex Murphy on Bradford's signing

The Life Of Foster

Trevor Foster, a driving force behind the resurrection of Bradford Northern in the 1960s also played the role of Jesus Christ in a 1956 floodlit pageant called 'The Life Of Christ'.

Get A Real Job

The Northern Union only legalised professionalism in 1898, but then also laid down some strict regulations, including a clause on employment. It stated that all professional players must be in 'bona fide' employment. Non bona fide methods of employment included billiard markers and public house waiters.

MacFlop

In 1953 Leigh took the ambitious move of signing West Indian sprinter E MacDonald Bailey. There was no doubt about Bailey's pace, but he did not readily make the jump from track to rugby field, and in fact only played one game for Leigh before quitting the game due to injury.

Carry Out

At the turn of the century, rugby balls were more rounded in shape, and actually had carrying handles.

Tickets, Please

How many times after a great sporting event do people say 'I was there?' Well, with the Challenge Cup Final of 1954 at Odsal, Bradford, believe anyone who says it. Over 100,000 spectators flooded into the ground, a former corporation rubbish tip, to watch Warrington narrowly   beat Halifax.

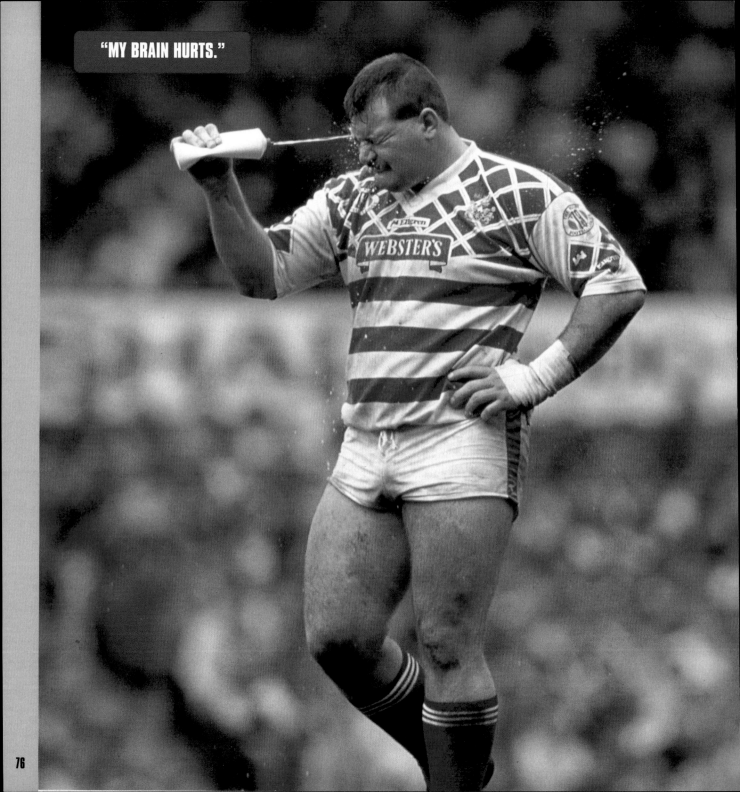

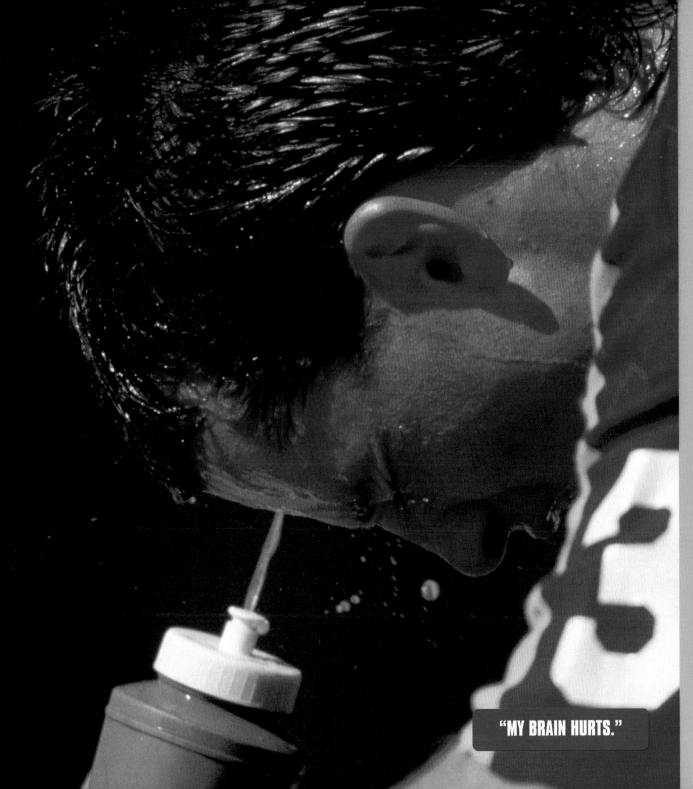

"MY BRAIN HURTS."

77

Pay For Play

Northern rugby clubs began the practice of paying players 'broken time' money – payments for playing rugby because players would have to forego some of their working day, and wages, to be able to play in a match.

'And he's got the icepack on the groin there, so possibly not the old shoulder injury.'
TV commentator Ray French

Give That Man A Cigar

One of the early scourges of professionalism in rugby was the Reverend Francis Marshall. He was also a referee, who often used to enjoy a cigar while taking charge of a match.

"HE'S BEHIND YOU!"
"OH NO HE ISN'T!"
"OH YES I F**K**G AM!"

That's 13 Cigars And A Tub Of Deep Heat?

The early days of rugby saw great suspicion of 'professionalism' even though payments to players were made. Clubs found interesting ways of raising and accounting for money used to fund players. For example, an entry in the books of the Leeds Parish Church rugby club shows payments for champagne, supper and cigars, plus a night of entertainment at the theatre and a river cruise. Coincidentally, the club had an away fixture in Liverpool.

> 'Peter Sterling:
> If Walt Disney had seen this little man's antics there would have been no Mickey Mouse.'
> Ray French

> 'It's the first time I've been cold for seven years. I was never cold playing rugby league.'
> Jonathan Davies on his return to Union in 1995

Numbers Game

The final straw that persuaded northern clubs to break from the Rugby Football Union in London was when an edict by the RFU effectively outlawed games with less than 15 players a side, knowing that the northern clubs were keen to reduce the number of players in a team to 13.

Which Game Do You Fancy Playing?

The first winners of the new Northern Union Championship, which commenced in 1895-96, were Manningham. They won 33 of their 42 games. It was to be a short zenith for the Bradford-based club though, just a few years later they were forced to abandon rugby league for financial reasons and turn instead to soccer, where they became Bradford City FC.

"YOU WANT TO GET THOSE ROOTS DYED."

"RIGHT NO.7, FIVE MINUTES IN THE SILLY HAIRSTYLE SIN BIN."

> 'The crowd were really given their money's worth today. They saw two games ... one when Britain had the ball and another when Australia had it.'
> (Australia beat Britain 4 0-4 in 1982)

First Cup

The first Challenge Cup competition was played in 1897. The first trophy cost £60 and was made by Fattorini & Sons.

Love Is In The Air

Albert Rosenfeld was a member of the first Australian team to set foot on British soil in 1908, and it took him 55 years to ever go back down under. He fell in love with a Huddersfield girl and then signed to play for her club. He twice topped the English try scoring charts.

Percentage Play

For the 1905-06 season, a league of 31 clubs was formed, and teams were told to complete a minimum of 20 games in the season, with no limit on the total of fixtures played above that number. The winner of the league title was then decided on who had the best percentage record overall. Champions Leigh played 30 games overall, while Oldham finished fourth having played 40 games.

Happy Landings

In the first Challenge Cup Final, Batley fly-half Oakland dropped a goal to give his side an early lead against St Helens. One spectator at the Headingley ground, perched in a tree for a better view, was so overcome by the excitement of the score that he fell out of his vantage point. It was the only time a drop goal was worth four points in the Cup Final.

Where Did He Go?

Billy Batten of Hunslett developed an interesting way of evading tackles after seeing a Maori player perform the same trick in 1910. He took to hurdling the tackler just as the opponent committed himself. His sons played rugby league, too, and they also inherited their dad's quirky style of beating opponents.

Bridging The Gap

Chelsea Football Club's home ground of Stamford Bridge was used to stage the second Test Match between the Northern Union and the touring New Zealanders in 1908.

What Do You Think, Mum?

The great Australian player of the early 1900s, Dally Messenger, officially turned professional on the formation of the New South Wales Rugby League in 1907. He was offered £180 to do so – a sum which he accepted, but only after he had consulted with his mother.

> 'Putting Maurice Lindsay in the super hero role clearly indicated that Super League was in trouble.'
> Danny Weidler, Sports Monthly

Wheeler Dealer

Scotsman John Wilson became the first paid official of the Northern Union in 1920. On his CV Wilson also had the fact that he had represented his country at cycling in the 1912 Stockholm Olympics.

Grand Game

In 1921, Leeds paid the first £1,000 transfer fee for winger Harold Buck of Hunslet.

New Look

The Rugby Football League was formed in 1922 when Northern Union officials decided a new identity was required for the sport.

> 'There are too many soft-cocks in rugby league who only say what people want to hear.'
> Bozo Fulton, rugby coach

Radio Days

The 1927 Challenge Cup final at Wigan, between Oldham and Swinton, was the first time the match had been broadcast on the radio. The Final moved to Wembley in 1929.

Ton Up Lomas

Utility back James Lomas became the first £100 transfer player in 1901 when he moved from Bramley to Salford.

Rationed Out

The playing of rugby league was outlawed in France under the Petain government of World War II. Rugby Union, however, was not affected.

What's In A Name

Just after World War II the French rugby union authorities succeeded in placing copyright on the word 'rugby' which meant that the French rugby league authorities had to change their name, and the game became Jeu a XIII as opposed to Rugby a XIII.

> 'To play rugby league, you need three things: a good pass, a good tackle and a good excuse.'
> Anon

McKivat's Rules

Australian captain in 1911, Chris McKivat, was a well respected player – when he spoke players listened. If they didn't, they realised it quickly. McKivat once had occasion to speak sternly to one of his forwards who was scrummaging illegally. The forward didn't heed the warning, and received a swift kick up the backside from his captain for his troubles.

Do We Have To Play Them?

One of the dominant teams of the early 20th century was Huddersfield. Their points tally for the 1914-15 season read: points for 1,269; points against 286.

Where Are We?

For the 1931 season, a complicated league formula was set up divided between the two counties of Lancashire and Yorkshire. To even the number of teams up, Halifax had to become honorary members of Lancashire, although they were still allowed to play in the Yorkshire Cup.

Time For A Break

French full-back and captain Puig-Aubert was a mercurial talent, but not without vices. He would very often cadge a cigarette or a swig of beer off a spectator during quiet periods of a game.

Eddie's Troops

Eddie Waring, TV commentator, game show host and man responsible for having thousands of kids incessantly shouting: 'It's an up and under' when playing rugby in the street, actually came in to rugby league management at the age of 26 when he took over the hot seat at Dewsbury.

Who's Best

Two inter-code games were played during World War II – a League side registering two wins over a Union side, despite the matches being played to Union rules.

Next Stop Hollywood

Cash for rugby league was short between the Wars, but Featherstone Rovers found an enterprising way of putting some extra pounds in the coffers. The Rovers' ground, some of its players and fans appeared in the film 'The Hope Of The Side' made in 1935.

Jim's Switch

Wigan's prodigious goal kicker of the 1920s and 1930s, Jim Sullivan, also had the distinction of having represented Wales at baseball.

Anyone Seen The Paint Brush?

Leeds played Wigan in December 1932, in one of the first games to be played under floodlights. There were a few technical difficulties, including the need to regularly replace the ball, whitewashed to show up under the lights, because the paint kept wearing off.

Wait 'Til You Try To Leave

Sunday matches were sanctioned by the RFL in 1967, but ingenious methods of charging spectators to watch had to be found to circumvent the law. Spectators outside the ground would be charged for a programme or a leaflet advertising the game and then let in to watch free of charge.

'Rugby league is a game of grit and passion. It was born out of controversy and has had its fair share of ups and downs ever since. Yet nothing has stopped its popularity growing from those small beginnings in the north of England.'
Rodney Walker – RFL

"COME HERE, YOU SEXY THING!"

Lost Their Shirts

Rugby league was a cash-strapped game in the early 1970s. So much so that British players who swapped shirts with their French counterparts after a close international game in 1972 found £5 deducted from their £30 match fee.

Who's Got The Cup

Australia won the World Cup in 1970, beating Britain in the play-off final. During the celebrations, though, the trophy disappeared, and didn't turn up again for 20 years, when it was found in a ditch a few miles from the team hotel.

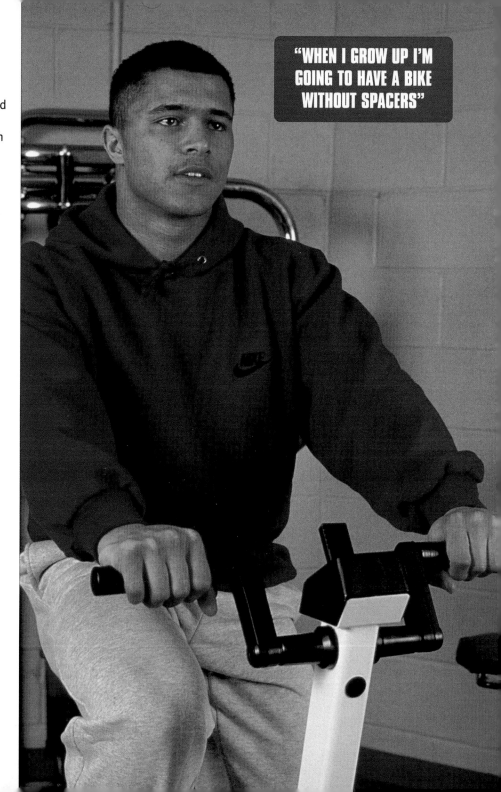

"WHEN I GROW UP I'M GOING TO HAVE A BIKE WITHOUT SPACERS"

Good Job They Flew

The 1971 New Zealand touring party to Britain was captained by Roy Christian – a descendant of the Mr Christian who led the mutiny on the Bounty.

Brave Name?

Wigan's first ground was called Folly Field.

It Was A Gift, Honest

In November 1908, Wigan obtained a summons against a Mr Edward Croston, a local businessman, who had made an attempt to bribe two Wigan players with a view to influencing the result of a game. Croston was convicted and excluded from all Northern Union grounds.

Lights, Action!

In 1966 the BBC introduced a new competition to rugby league with the BBC2 Floodlit Trophy. Matches were played under lights during the week and televised. Not all clubs were able to take part – for example Wigan did not have floodlights and therefore were excluded from the first tournament. The following year Wigan installed lights at a cost of £17,500 and inaugurated them with a match against Bradford Northern in September 1967. Unfortunately the lights failed twice during the game. There is a happy ending, though. Wigan won the BBC2 Floodlit Trophy the following season in 1969.

Ever-present Len

Len Mason played in 118 consecutive games for Wigan between August 1927 and December 1929.

'Gareth Edwards. The sooner that little so-and-so goes to rugby league the better it will be for all of us.'
Dickie Jeeps, 1967

'St Helens have really got their tails between their teeth.'
Malcolm Lord

Capital Idea, Not

The touring Australian team of 1973/74 requested a switch of venues for the first Test against Britain, believing they would get greater support from the Australian population in London if the game was held at Wembley rather than Wigan's Central Park. A good idea in principle, but less than 10,000 actually turned up at Wembley to watch the game.

Working Both Sides

Welshman John Devereux made history in 1996 by becoming the first player to sign a deal to play rugby league in the summer, with Widnes, and rugby union in the winter, with Sale.

Fed Up With Eddie

A petition of some 10,000 signatures was once handed to the BBC demanding the removal of Eddie Waring from the BBC commentary team because his commentaries were insulting and had turned the game into something of a music hall joke.

Holiday Affair

Widnes coach Doug Laughton had a shrewd eye for a potential league player. Watching a rugby match on television while holed up in an Anglesey caravan park he saw Tongan player Emosi Koloto play for Wellington in New Zealand against a touring Welsh team. Laughton had no idea what the TV pundits were saying about the big number 8 because the commentary was in Welsh, but he saw enough of the action to telephone the Tongan, persuade him he had a future with Widnes and then sign him.

Union Thrashed

League clashed with Union again in 1996 when Wigan took on the dominant team in the 15-a-side code, Bath. A game under Union rules saw Bath run out winners by 44-19, but a previous game under League rules had seen Wigan trounce Bath 82-6. Just to add insult to Union injury, Wigan also won the Middlesex 7s tournament that year.

Royal Rhinos

Leeds Rhinos pre-season training for the 1998 season involved a December visit to a Royal Marines Commando centre where they set about learning unarmed combat as well as attempting endurance training and fearsome assault courses.

JASON PUTTING ON HIS NEW HAT

Sing It, Don't Kick It

The 1995 Rugby league World Cup was officially opened by singer Diana Ross. Only a year previously Ms Ross had opened the World Cup soccer tournament in the USA, but had somehow failed to hit an open goal from the penalty spot as a crucial part of the opening ceremony. Wisely, the rugby league organisers declined the soul singing Diva a chance to further embarrass herself by kicking at goal with an oval ball.

> 'We've said it once, we've said it many times. There's no excuse for pace.'
> Alex Murphy

Winning Habit

In 1972 Australian side Cessnock won their first league title for some 12 years, but they may have some help from a greater force. Coach Norm Henderson made great use of the steep bank of 80 steps leading up to the Cessnock convent in his training schedule for the players. Every now and then the local nuns would come out to lend their encouragement to the players puffing up and down the steps. And then Cessnock won the league. Coincidence?

Get Your Hair Cut

In a bid to seemingly keep standards high within its walls, the Eastern Suburbs Leagues Club in Sydney, the Club's laws included a clause that stated no male member or visitor, including players, would be permitted entry if their hair was long enough to pass over their collar.

Diddums

His schoolmasterly method of refereeing did not endear Keith Page to members of the North Sydney team during a match against Canterbury in 1970. Four Sydney players walked off the pitch in a rage complaining that Page was intent on humiliating them by treating them like children.

"WHICH ONE SHOULD I TACKLE?"

"I'LL HAVE YOU KNOW, OLD CHAP, THAT I'M AT THE CUTTING EDGE OF FASHION IN SALFORD."

Brace Yourself, Sheila

The Australian team of 1972 prepared meticulously for its Test match with New Zealand, including six days in a training camp where it was just players and coaching staff together. Centre Bobby Fulton conceded that such arrangements had drawbacks: 'I suppose the first question you ask is about the sex life. We don't have time to worry about sex. Our mind is fully occupied with the Test. We know we are in camp for one purpose – to win the Test. Sex just has to take a back seat for six days.'

Now Bark Like Dogs

Australian side Canterbury found that desperate measures sometimes work as they looked to find a way of ending a five week slump in the 1975 season. The Canterbury team took to the field for a game against Newtown having been hypnotised. They won, too.

Ride 'Em Cowboy

Queensland second row forward Forrester Grayson quit the macho life of rugby league in 1978 to take residence in the even manlier world of the cowboy. Grayson hung up his boots and donned his spurs to make a career as a full-time rodeo rider.

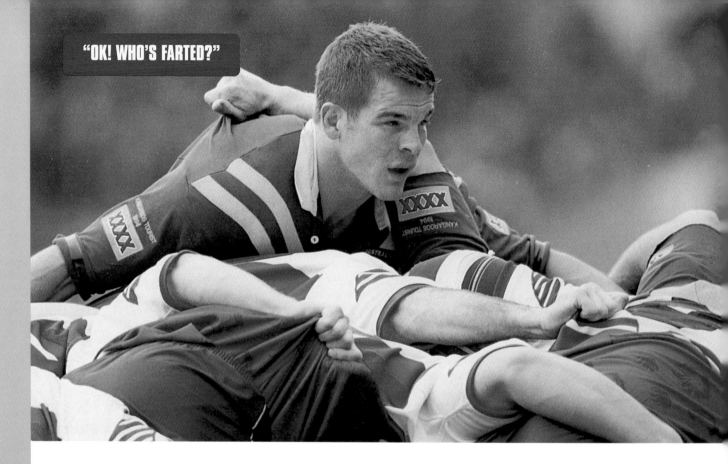

"OK! WHO'S FARTED?"

Burglary Free Household

Mr and Mrs Kevin Walters have reason to be proud parents. Their brood of five sons have all, at some time, played representative rugby for their native Queensland state team.

Tragic Story

Newtown half-back Paul Hayward's rugby career finished in October 1978 when he was arrested in Bangkok for possession of over 8kg of heroin and sentenced to 20 years in prison. Hayward was released in 1989 after it was confirmed he had AIDS, and he died in Australia in 1992.

Tina

Rocking grandma Tina Turner was signed up by the New South Wales League to front a promotional campaign for the game. She also opened the 1993 grand final in suitably rock fashion by belting out a hit to the thousands present.

Once Bitten...

Western Suburbs captain Tommy Raudonikis found himself in trouble after a front page article in Australian paper Rugby League Week exposed him as 'The Phantom Biter' in a piece apparently written by Raudonikis, who was a columnist for RLW.

Raudonikis had bitten opposing player John Gibbs on the nose in a game against Manly. Not only was Raudonikis banned by the authorities from writing for RLW again, he was also fined $200 (which the paper paid). Worse still, after being bitten on the hooter Gibbs went on to score two tries.

Tough On The Cat

Australian player David Howell, skipper of the Wests side, was the recipient of a bizarre death threat in 1981. Wests' president Geoff Wright found a dead cat on his doorstep. The cat had been shot between the eyes and attached to its body in a note compiled from newspaper cuttings was a message threatening Howell.

Away Strip

Darrell Smith spent his Sundays playing half back for amateur side Genelg in South Australia. And during the week Smith, under the nickname Dazzling Darrell, earned a living as a male stripper in the Penthouse Club disco in Adelaide.

In One Ear...

In a bid to improve their performance, the 1975 Manly-Warringah side of Australia listened keenly to a lecture about the benefits of vitamins and how a lack of sex could heighten an athlete's performance in a game. Did they take the advice on board or was it just tosh? Whatever, the club embarked on a multi-game losing streak immediately after the lecture.

SPICE GIRLS ARE US.

Girl Power

When Jamie Kahurkura's brother was unable to take his place in the team of Whakaki in New Zealand, it seemed only natural that the 16-year-old Jamie step into the breach and make a senior rugby league debut at the same time. But this was no ordinary occasion, because Jamie is a girl, although none of the opposing players of the Paikea Whalers realised this until after the game when Jamie took off her number six shirt to remove her borrowed shoulder pads.

Life, Death, Or More Important?

Australian halfback Ricky Stuart went from villain to hero in a 1990 Test match against Great Britain. With less than a quarter of the game to go, Stuart threw a risky pass which was intercepted by Britain centre Paul Loughlin who scored to level the game at 10-10. But in the last minute Stuart played a key role in a move which saw Mal Meninga seal another Australian win.

Said Stuart: 'The further I ran, the closer Mal got to me. In the end it was a simple matter of draw the fullback and pass. But during the run it seemed a million thoughts went through my head. I couldn't bear to think how I would feel if I bungled that one. My earlier blue (the intercept) was just like a death in the family.'

May The Best Side Draw

Newtown coach Warren Ryan unknowingly uttered prophetic words prior to a 1982 game with Canterbury. 'Canterbury are not like any other side in the competition. You can have them beaten territorially and technically. But the one place you may not have them beaten is on the scoreboard.'

After 80 minutes of a hard fought game, during which Newtown indeed did run Canterbury ragged, the final result read 0-0, the first such score in Australian premiership history. Ryan's reaction after the game? 'The better side drew,' he said.

Frilled To Meet You

When Australian Steve Georgallis arrived in Carlisle to join his new club, he found he already had a fan club. During negotiations prior to signing, a fax from his manager describing Georgallis as an Australian Rugby League legend had inadvertently found its way to a Carlisle lingerie shop rather than the club's office. Having read the fax, the three shop assistants rushed the message to the club and insisted Carlisle sign Georgallis so they could meet him.

Have We Started Yet?

The 1972 Challenge Cup final between Leeds and St Helens was a fast starting affair. Leeds hooker Tony Fisher threw a ball back but saw it collected by the opposition loose forward Graham Rees who galloped across the line to register the first score of the match. Only 35 seconds had elapsed since the kick-off.

> Peter Deakin when asked about the renaming of Bradford Northern to Bradford Bulls: 'Bradford is famous for sheep, but we didn't think that had quite the same ring. When we asked on local radio for a name with Yorkshire connotations, someone suggested puddings. So it's Bulls.'

You Taking The Piss?

Australian playmaker Wally Lewis pulled a fast one on the authorities when asked to submit a urine sample for random drug testing after a game in Brisbane in 1986. Lewis submitted a test tube containing flat lager beer, and received a clean bill of health from the testers.

Man Of Power

Super League chief Maurice Lindsay rated 12th out of the top-50 most powerful people in sport according to Total Sport magazine in 1996.

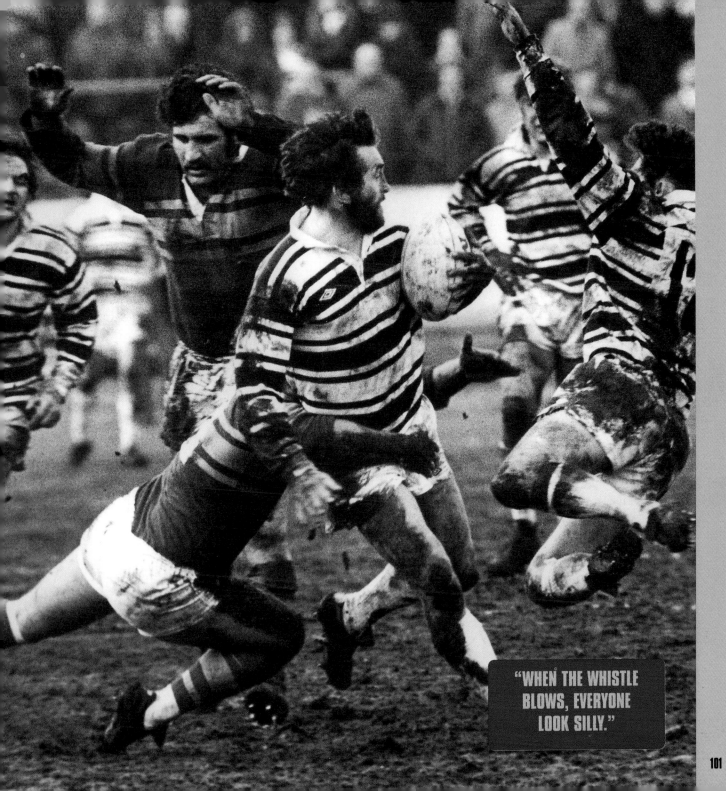

"WHEN THE WHISTLE BLOWS, EVERYONE LOOK SILLY."

"SORRY LADS, I'VE GOT LOOSE BOWELS."

And Offiah Must Score...D'Oh!

The 1990 tour of New Zealand was a triumphant one for Britain, despite touring with a squad weakened by high profile pull-outs, including that of captain and inspiration Ellery Hanley. Britain won two of the three Test matches, and would have made it a clean sweep but for a mighty blooper from Martin Offiah. With the try line wide open, Offiah somehow contrived to drop the ball, and Britain's winning chance in the game.

Rubbing It In

Alex Murphy's St Helens team beat Wigan in the 1966 Challenge Cup final, enough to tempt the mischievous Murphy into sending a telegram to the beaten Wigan team saying: 'Roses are red, violets are blue, St Helens 21, Wigan 2.'

Saints March On

St Helens won the first Super League Championship in 1996, beating Warrington 66-14 and thus pipping Wigan by a single point for the title. In all, St Helens won 20 of their 22 Super League fixtures, and added the Challenge Cup trophy to the cabinet in the same season.

Should Have Left A Tip

Bobby Goulding's wild-child reputation was born in 1990 when the 18-year-old was touring New Zealand with the Great Britain squad. After less than a week on Kiwi soil, Goulding found himself on assault charges following a fracas in an Auckland restaurant. He was let off, but had to fork out £165 to each of the two people who had lodged a complaint against him.

Luxury

Details in the document 'Framing The Future' which set out the plans for Super League, also specified that working journalists would have a minimum of 600mm working space at matches, and fans would never have to walk further than 60 metres to the nearest toilet.

Ian's Outing

North Queensland's Ian Roberts, renowned as one of the game's hard men, startled the rugby league world by declaring his homosexuality via his posing semi-naked on a magazine cover under the headline 'Meet The Man I Love'. Not that many people would dare question his motives face to face.

Every One An XL

The 1990 French team signed up a new shirt sponsor, Jiffi condoms.

'Rugby league is dead in England... It's dead in New Zealand... And there's none in France. And if it's not in a healthy position in Australia, it's dead. This is going to kill it. So there's got to be a compromise.'
Australian Rugby League's Graham Richardson on the civil war in his country's game.

In Case Of Fire

Maurice Lindsay rated pretty low in the popularity stakes when the arrival of Super League was announced, and along with it the possible closure of long established clubs. One story has it that Mr Lindsay had to double the fire insurance on his home... just in case.

SUCH SWEET BOYS.

Lovesick For Leeds

New Zealander Richie Blackmore played four seasons for Castleford before heading back to his home country to play for Auckland. However, his Leeds-born wife couldn't settle down under and Blackmore took up an offer to return to play in England, to his wife's hometown club in fact, in order to protect his marriage.

> 'You've never been in front in any of the matches you've played, but you've always come out the winners.'
> Alex Murphy

Murphy's Law

St Helens star Alex Murphy played a major role in the changing of the penalty laws through his tactics of persistent infringement in the 1966 Challenge Cup Final. With Saints opponents Wigan lacking a regular hooker, Murphy realised that possession from scrummages was virtually guaranteed. So he continually played offside, conceded penalties which were kicked to touch, and from the ensuing scrum Saints duly won the ball back. Such dubious tactics contributed hugely to Saints' 21-2 win. The RFL then decided at a meeting to change the law to a tap kick to the non-offending team rather than a scrum after a penalty was kicked to touch.

He Feels No Pain

When Alex Murphy took to the pitch for the 1974 Challenge Cup Final, this time wearing the colours of Warrington, it was his fifth Wembley appearance, and to that point he was unbeaten. He was a key component to a re-emerging Warrington team, and his presence on the pitch was vital. However, with 10 minutes to go before half-time, Murphy had to leave the field with injured ribs and, come the interval, Warrington trailed Featherstone 9-8. During the break, Murphy received five pain killing injections, and then played the second half, eventually guiding Warrington to a 24-9 victory.

Help!

The committee at Salford must know how the man who turned down The Beatles felt. They took too long deliberating over the signature of Andy Gregory, despite being the team that 'discovered' the man who went on to be a major world star in rugby league. While the Salford committee talked, Widnes coach Doug Laughton did – sign the young Gregory, that is.

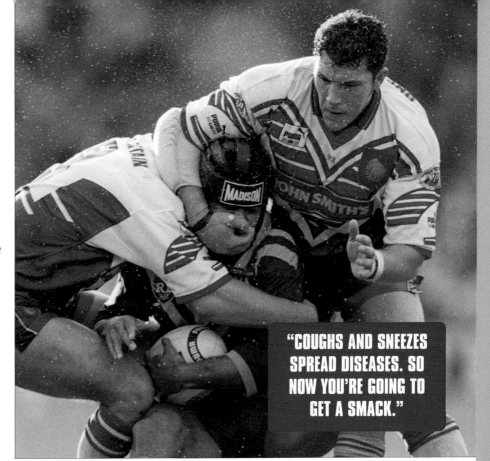

"COUGHS AND SNEEZES SPREAD DISEASES. SO NOW YOU'RE GOING TO GET A SMACK."

No-one Mentioned Rugby

Ellery Hanley joined his first rugby league club, Bradford Northern, before he had apparently even seen the game being played.

Fear Of Flying In

Castleford's Aboriginal star at half-back, Jamie Sandy, almost didn't take up a position with the club that won the Challenge Cup, with his help, in 1986. A fear of hijacking and terrorism in Europe almost persuaded Sandy to stay at home.

PLEASE DON'T FART!

PLEASE

PLEASE

PLEASE DON'T FART!

DON'T FART!

IF YOU ENJOYED THIS BOOK, WHAT ABOUT THESE!

All these books are available at your local book shop or can be ordered direct from the publisher.
Just list the titles you require and give your name address, including postcode.
Prices and availability are subject to change without notice.

Please send to Chameleon Cash Sales, 76 Dean Street, London W1V 5HA, a cheque or postal
order for £7.99 and add the following for postage and packaging:
UK - £1.00 For the first book, 50p for the second and 30p for the third and for each additional
book up to a maximum of £3.00.
OVERSEAS - (including Eire) £2.00 For the first book, £1.00 for the second and 50p for each
additional book up to a maximum of £3.00.